101
Bug Jokes

BY LISA EISENBERG & KATY HALL

ILLUSTRATED BY DON OREHEK

SCHOLASTIC INC.
New York Toronto London Auckland Sydney

To
TED EISENBUG
and
GERM McMULLAN

Cover illustration by Robert DeMichiell.

ISBN 0-590-99818-8

24 23 22 21 20 19 18 17   5 6 7 8/0

Printed in the U.S.A.   01

STEP ON IT!

What happened to the two bedbugs
who fell in love?

They were married in the spring!

What do you call little bugs that live
on the moon?

Luna ticks!

Why did the Las Vegas moth eat a hole in the rug?

He wanted to see the floor show!

Why do spiders spin webs to catch flies?

Because they don't know how to knit!

If there are five flies in the kitchen,
which one is the cowboy?

The one on the range!

GET THE POINT?

What is a mosquito's favorite sport?

Skin diving!

What kind of boats do mosquitoes like best?

Blood vessels!

What kind of paper do mosquitoes like?

Scratch paper!

Why are mosquito families so close?

Because blood is thicker than water!

Why was the little mosquito up so late?

He had to study for his blood test!

LIGHT MOMENTS

How do you start a firefly race?

On your mark, get set, glow!

How did the firefly feel when it ran into the fan?

It was de-lighted!

What did the mommy lightning bug
say to the daddy lightning bug?

"Junior certainly is bright!"

What did one lightning bug say to
the other?

*"What time are you going out
tonight?"*

What goes snap, crackle, fizz?

A firefly with a short circuit!

Some boy scouts from the city were sitting around their campfire. One scout said, "We'd better get to bed before the mosquitoes eat us up."

Later that night, the boy woke up and looked out of his tent. He saw dozens and dozens of fireflies. Quickly, he woke up his friends and said, "We'd better hide! They're coming after us with flashlights!"

BUGLAND'S MUSICAL GROUPS AND STARS

Dur-ant Dur-ant

Michael Jackstung

Lionel R-itchy

The Bee-tles

Jose Flea-ciano

Pat Bugatar

Gnat King Cole

Bruce Stingsteen

BUZZ-ZZZ

Why did the bee go to the doctor?

It had hives!

How do bees make money?

They cell their honey!

What did the bee say to the flower?

"Hi, Bud! What time do you open?"

What did the flower say to the bee?

"Buzz off!"

What creature is smarter than a talking parrot?

A spelling bee!

A BEE'S TV GUIDE

Daytime

2:00: Days of Our Hives
3:00: The Edge of Flight

Evening

5:00: Carol Bee-Net
5:30: Hardy Bees Mystery
6:00: ABeeC News
NBeeC News
CBeeS News
6:30: Barna-bee Jones
Starring Buggy Ebsen
7:00: Leave It to Bee-ver
7:30: Bee-Haw
8:00: Bee's Company
8:30: The A-Team
9:00: The Bee-Team
9:30: Hawaii Hive-O

TAKE A SWAT
AT THESE!

What has four legs and catches flies?

Two outfielders!

What has no wings, but flies all over?

A spider!

What has four wheels and flies?

A garbage truck!

What is green and slimy, has 12 legs, hairy feelers, and wings?

I don't know, but there's one crawling up your shoulder!

What kind of fly has a frog in its throat?

A hoarse (horse) fly!

What did the fly say to the fly paper?

"I'm stuck on you!"

Why did the fly fly?

Because the spider spied her!

Knock, knock.
Who's there?
Hewlette.
Hewlette who?

Hewlette all the flies in the house?

BUG OFF!

Why are frogs so happy?

They eat whatever bugs them!

What's the quickest way for a bug to get from the ground to a tree trunk?

Take the shortest root!

Why wouldn't they let the stinkbug into the movie?

He had only one scent (cent) — and it wasn't enough!

What is a bug after it is four days old?

Five days old!

HILL-ARIOUS!

Which ant lives in a house?

Occup__ant__!

Which ant is an army officer?

Serge__ant__!

Which is the biggest ant?

Gi<u>ant</u>!

Which is the second biggest ant?

Eleph<u>ant</u>!

Which is the bossiest ant?

Tyr<u>ant</u>!

Which is the dumbest ant?

Ignorant!

JUST JOKING!

Little boy: Daddy, are bugs good to eat?

Father: Let's not talk about that at the table, son.

(after dinner)

Father: Now, son, what did you want to ask me?

Little boy: Oh nothing. There was a bug in your soup — but now it's gone!

Dave: Did you hear about the dog that went to the flea circus?

Jim: No, what happened?

Dave: He stole the show!

Teacher: Jimmy, spell *wasp*.

Jimmy: W–A–S.

Teacher: But what's at the end?

Jimmy: The stinger!

City Visitor: I never saw so many flies! Don't you shoo them?

Farmer: No, we just let them go barefoot!

BUGGY HIT PARADE

Let It Bee
   by Sting

I've Got You Under My Skin
   by Mick Jabber

Fly Me to the Moon
   by Paul McCartney & Wings

Singing in the Vein
   by Blood, Sweat & Tears

SCRATCHING FOR LAUGHS!

Why was the mother flea so upset?

All her children were going to the dogs!

How do you start a flea market?

You start from scratch!

What is the difference between a dog and a flea?

A dog can have fleas, but a flea can't have dogs!

What did the hungry flea say to his friend?

Let's go out for a bite!

What do you call a rabbit with fleas?

Bugs Bunny!

What did one flea say to the other
when they came out of the movies?

"Shall we walk, or take a dog?"

BUGS! BUGS! BUGS!

What do you call nervous insects?

Jitterbugs!

What do you call a bug that hates Christmas?

A humbug!

Which bug gobbles up trash?

The litterbug!

Which bug lives at the top of a house?

A tick (attic)!

Which bug does amazing motorcycle stunts?

Evel Boll Weevil!

LEGGO!

What's worse than a giraffe with a sore throat?

A centipede with bunions!

What's worse than an octopus with tennis elbow?

A centipede with athlete's foot!

What did the centipede say to the
shoe salesman?

*"I need a new pair of shoes, new pair
of shoes, new pair of shoes. . . ."*

What did the girl centipede say to
the boy centipede at the dance?

*"You're stepping on my foot, my foot,
my foot. . . ."*

THE BEST OF BUGGY TV

Fly Witness News

Dy-gnat-sy

Web-ster

Family Flies

Gimme a Buzz

Knight Spider

WHO'S THERE?

Knock, knock.
Who's there?
Roach.
Roach who?
Roach you a letter — did you get it?

Knock, knock.
Who's there?
Weevil.
Weevil who?
Weevil see you real soon!

Knock, knock.
Who's there?
Tick.
Tick who?
Ticklish, aren't you?

Knock, knock.
Who's there?
Spider.
Spider who?
Spider just behind those bushes!

CRAZY CROSSES

What do you get if you cross a bee
with a firearm?

A Bee-Bee gun!

What do you get if you cross a beetle
with a Rolling Stone?

A squashed bug!

What do you get if you cross a beetle
with a ghost?

A bugaboo!

What do you get if you cross a beetle
with a mistake?

A bugaboo-boo!

What do you get if you cross a mosquito with an elephant?

I don't know, but if it stings you, you're in big trouble!

What do you get if you cross a spider with an elephant?

Who knows? But when it crawls across your ceiling, the roof will collapse!

YIKES!

How can you make a tarantula float?

Two scoops of ice cream, some chocolate syrup, and a tarantula on top!

How can you make a tarantula shake?

Run up behind it and say, "BOO!"

What's the best way to talk to a tarantula?

Long distance!

What is a tarantula's favorite apple drink?

Spider cider!

Ted: What would you do if you saw a big, hairy tarantula?

Jim: Hope it didn't see *me!*

WAITER, WAITER

Diner: Waiter! What's this fly doing in my alphabet soup?

Waiter: Learning to read, sir!

Diner: Waiter! There's a fly in my soup!

Waiter: Don't worry, sir. He won't eat much!

Diner: What's this fly doing in my soup?

Waiter: Looks like the backstroke, sir!

Diner: Waiter! There's a fly in my chow mein!

Waiter: That's nothing. Wait till you see what's in your fortune cookie!

BUG FUN

What do you call two spiders that just got married?

Newly webs!

What's the best way to prevent
infections caused by biting insects?

Don't bite any insects!

What are the most faithful bugs?

*Ticks. They always stick to their
friends!*

What well-known cartoon character
do moths like a *hole* lot?

Mickey Moth!

What kind of shoes do bees take a shine to?

Buzz-ter Browns, of course!

CREEPY CRAWLERS

What TV show do mosquitoes avoid?

The SWAT Team!

What TV show do ants hate to watch?

*M*A*S*H!*

What would happen if a Black Widow spider fell into the Red Sea?

She'd get wet!

How does a caterpillar start the day?

It turns over a new leaf!

Why did the girl spray her clock?

It was full of ticks!

UN-BEE-LIEVABLE
RIDDLES

What dance do bees really go for?

The Bee-bop!

What do you get when you cross a bee with a quarter-pound of ground beef?

A humburger!

What do you call a bee that can't make up his mind?

A maybee!

Why are letter A's like flowers?

Because B's come after them!

A TRICKY, ICKY TONGUE TWISTER

(Try it!)

Blue black bug's blood.

Now say it five times fast!

A HOLE LOT
OF LAUGHS

What insect lives on next to nothing?

The moth — it always eats holes!

What do you call a female moth?

A myth! (miss)

Which bugs talk too much?

Moths. They're always chewing the rag!

If a moth breathes oxygen in the daytime, what does it breathe at night?

Nightrogen (nitrogen)!

Do moths cry?

Yes. Haven't you ever seen a moth bawl?

BUG WUGS

What do you call an insect's
embrace?

A bug hug!

What do you call an insect's
trousers?

Ant's pants!

What do you call an insect-flavored
soup?

Moth broth!

What do you call an overly confident insect?

A smug bug!

BEE-WARE

Why is a bee like an insult?

Because both carry a sting!

How are a doorbell and a bee alike?

They're both buzzers!

Where did Noah keep his bees?

In the ark hives (archives)!

How can you tell a literary bee?

He's always quoting "Two bees or not two bees," from Shakespeare's play, Humlet.

TENT TALK

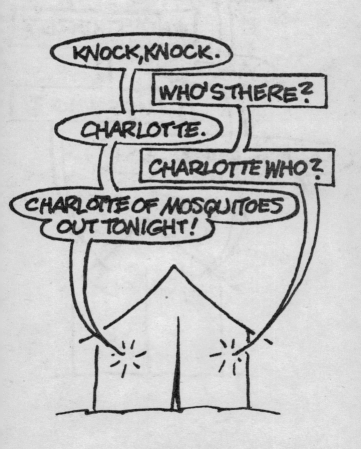

WHAT? WHAT? WHAT?

What looks just like half a butterfly?

The other half!

What letter can sting you?

B, of course!

What do hornets have that no other insects have?

Baby hornets!

What famous baseball player drives
bugs batty?

Mickey Mantis!

What's faster than a speeding bullet
and eats buildings in a single bite?

Super Termite!

ITCHING FOR FUN

Where do mosquitoes keep their money?

In a bloodbank!

What did the mosquito say to the girl after it bit her arm?

*"You're just my type — **A** positive!"*

What kind of cars do mosquitoes drive?

Bloodmobiles!

Did you hear about the Romeo and Juliet mosquitoes?

They loved in vein (vain)!

How can you tell when there's a mosquito in your bed?

By the "M" on its pajamas!

Two mosquitoes were having a chat on Robinson Crusoe's back. One said to the other, "I have to go now. But let's meet again on Friday!"

CELEBUGGIES

What comedian do termites really eat up?

Woody Allen, of course!

Robert Redford starred in *The Sting,* but who should have gotten the lead?

Warren Bee-ty!

Why do spiders enjoy watching *Dragnet*?

They love its star, Jack Web!

Why is *Maude* a big hit in the hive?

Because it stars Bee Arthur!

Who starred in *Tootsie*?

Who else? Du-sting Hoffman!

Who is a bee-g star in the
N.BEE.A.? (NBA)

Kareem Abdul-Jabber!

ANTS! ANTS! ANTS!

Two ants were running across the top of a cereal box. One stopped and said to the other, "Hey, why are we running so fast?"

"Didn't you read what it says here?" answered the other ant. *"Tear across the dotted line!"*

Fred: This is an ideal spot for a picnic.

Judy: It must be. All these ants can't be wrong!

Teacher: Billy, define *buoyant*.

Billy: A male insect!

BUGGIE WUGGIES

What do you call an insect that's been hit over the head and robbed?

A mugged bug!

What do you call an insect that chooses its victims very, very carefully?

A picky tick-y!

What do you call a tarantula that's been traveling in a bunch of bananas?

A spider rider!

What do you call a tarantula that can't stay on a diet?

A wider spider!

What do you call a tarantula that's been on a diet?

A lighter spider!

ODDS 'N' ENDS

Why did the grasshopper go to the doctor?

Because he felt jumpy!

Why did the little dog almost itch to death?

He was so gentle, he wouldn't hurt a flea!

What does a queen bee use to part her hair?

A honeycomb!

Where can spiders always find a fly?

In Web-ster's Dictionary!

What has eight legs and a fast draw?

Billy the Squid!

Hey! What's a dumb squid joke doing
in this book?

We just stuck it in to <u>bug</u> you!